This
book
belongs to:

Richie Dutka

DANIEL BOONE

GREAT TALES FROM LONG AGO
DANIEL BOONE

Torstar Books Inc, 41 Madison Avenue, Suite 2900,
New York, NY 10010.
Copyright © 1985, Raintree Publishers Inc.

Library of Congress Cataloging in Publication Data
Gleiter, Jan, 1947-
  Daniel Boone.

  (Great tales from long ago)
  Summary: A biography of the legendary hero of the
American frontier, emphasizing his skill as a woodsman,
exploration of the Cumberland Gap, and relationship with
native Americans.
  1. Boone, Daniel, 1734-1820 – Juvenile literature.
2. Pioneers – Kentucky – Biography – Juvenile literature.
3. Frontier and pioneer life – Kentucky – Juvenile
literature. 4. Kentucky – Biography – Juvenile literature.
[1. Boone, Daniel, 1734-1820. 2. Pioneers.
3. Frontier and pioneer life – Kentucky] I. Thompson,
Kathleen. II. Tryon, Leslie, ill. III. Title.
IV. Series.
[F454.B66G57 1986] 976.9′02′0924 [9B] ·[92] 85-28883

ISBN 1-55001-036-0 (Great Tales from Long Ago Series)
ISBN 1-55001-016-6 (Daniel Boone)
10 9 8 7 6 5 4 3 2
Printed in Belgium

Great Tales from Long Ago
DANIEL BOONE

Jan Gleiter and Kathleen Thompson

Illustrated by Leslie Tryon

TORSTAR BOOKS

NEW YORK · TORONTO

The America of colonial times was a wild and wonderful place. But the beauty of Kentucky was legendary, even then. There were mountains, like the mountains of Virginia and the Carolinas. In Kentucky, though, the mountains were alive with animals. There were forests, like the forests of Pennsylvania and Vermont. But in Kentucky, the trees grew thick and tall, and there were clear spaces that seemed to be carpeted with wildflowers.

On the far side of the mountains, the land rolled gently. The streams were filled with fish. The sky was filled with birds. The woods were filled with wild turkeys, deer, elk, bears, and raccoons. And there were bison. There were so many bison that they seemed to be a dark, rolling cloud on the ground.

Kentucky belonged to the Indians. It was for hunting. No white settlers lived there. And those that did come didn't stay. Each spring, hunting parties from many Indian tribes came from all around. White hunters were not allowed.

Two men sat alone in a clearing under high trees. There was no campfire, because the smoke might have been seen by an Indian hunting party. And these men were not Indians. Their names were John Stuart and Daniel Boone.

When they started into the wilderness, there were four other men with them. The six of them had come through Cumberland Gap. That was a passage through the mountains. They had traveled far and hunted well.

But Indians had found their camp and had taken their furs and skins. The Indians had warned the hunters to leave the Indians' hunting ground.

"Well," said Daniel, "I'm not going. A man doesn't get a chance like this very often in his life."

"Nope," agreed John as he looked around. "I'm with you."

But the other four men had become discouraged, and they left.

S tuart and Boone stayed. But they were running out of supplies. They expected Daniel's brother Squire to bring what they needed. The trip was hard and dangerous. They hoped Squire would make it through.

A few days later, Squire found them. His horses were loaded with the things that they needed, especially bullets and gunpowder. Squire had also brought another hunter, Alexander Neeley.

It had been months since Daniel had seen his family. He missed his wife, Rebecca, and his children. His brother was someone from home. Seeing him made Daniel as happy as getting the supplies.

The four men divided into pairs to hunt. Daniel
went with John Stuart. Squire went with
Alexander Neeley.

None of them had ever seen a place like Kentucky.
It was so full of wildlife and so empty of people.

The pile of furs and skins at the camp grew. They
were very important because the Boones had
borrowed money from their neighbors to pay for the
trip. They would be able to sell the furs and skins
and pay back what they owed.

Everything was going very well. There did not
seem to be Indians anywhere.

One day, John Stuart went into the forest alone. He did not come back. Daniel looked for his friend for many days. Stuart was like another brother to him. Daniel went through the trees and into the deep gullies. He went along the creeks and streams. But he never found John Stuart. The wilderness could be a cruel place.

Alexander Neeley decided it was too cruel. "I'm leaving," he said. "I've had enough. I want to live to see my family again."

He went back to North Carolina and left the Boone brothers alone.

Squire and Daniel hunted until the pile of skins was almost too heavy for the horses to carry back to their home. Then Squire left with the valuable load. Daniel stayed, alone. Squire would return with more supplies.

While he waited for his brother, Daniel kept hunting. He knew that his family and his neighbors were counting on him.

Now, alone in the Kentucky wilderness, Daniel would need all of his skills as a woodsman.

Daniel knew the wilderness as well as the Indians knew it. He could move silently through the forest and leave no footprints. He could find food. He could find safe places for sleeping. Daniel almost seemed to be an Indian himself. There was a good reason for having Indian skills—Daniel had learned from the Indians themselves.

Daniel had grown up in a part of Pennyslvania where white settlers and Indians lived in peace. He had spent his childhood with Indian friends. Those friends had taught him how to read the tracks that animals left. They had taught him which berries were safe to eat, and how to live off the land. Daniel had learned how to hunt like an Indian, move like an Indian, and think like an Indian. He had learned his lessons well.

Squire came back at the end of July.

"Is Rebecca all right?" Daniel asked, the moment Squire reached the camp.

"Let me get off this horse, Daniel," Squire answered. "Then I'll tell you everything."

"The children?" Daniel went on, as his brother swung down.

"They're fine. Rebecca's fine. The skins are sold. Now can I sit down?" said Squire.

That night, the brothers built a fire and sat up late, talking. Daniel had been away from home for a long time. He was eager for news.

As winter got nearer, Squire went back again with another load of skins. And, again, Daniel stayed behind.

Was Daniel happy in the wilderness? It was lonely and dangerous. Yet, in a way, Daniel was always more at home in the woods than anywhere else.

One time, a group of men from Virginia were hunting in Kentucky. They were all good hunters and knew the wilderness well. Still, one afternoon they were badly frightened by a noise. They had never heard anything like it before.

Quickly they all hid, except for the leader. He moved from tree to tree, toward the noise. He thought that he would find a dying animal. But he did not.

What he found was a man, lying on a deerskin, singing loudly with joy. It was Daniel Boone. Squire came back one last time. He and Daniel joined the hunters from Virginia for a few months. The hunting went well. Finally, they loaded their horses and started for home.

D aniel had been warned more than once by the
  Indians: These were Indian lands. Everything
here—all the animals, all the skins—belonged to the
Indians. One day the Indians found the Boone
brothers.

   The Indians did not hurt the Boones. They warned
them again. And then they took the furs and skins.

After two years in the wilderness, Daniel Boone
went home, empty-handed. But he had
explored the land. He had named rivers and found
paths. One day he would return to Kentucky with
settlers. There would be a town named
Boonesborough. Then the wilderness would no
longer be a wilderness.

And Daniel Boone would move on.